Laughing It Off

The Low-Calorie Poem Diet

Rita Geil

Keep Laughing!

Rita Geil

Walnut Pond Press

Frenchtown, New Jersey

LAUGHING IT OFF-THE LOW-CALORIE POEM DIET is available at special quantity discounts for bulk purchases. For more information, please contact the Special Markets Department at Walnut Pond Press, 203 Main Street #325, Flemington, NJ 08825, phone (732) 220-6077, or visit the web site: www.laughingitoff.com.

Published by Walnut Pond Press
203 Main Street #325
Flemington, NJ 08822

Publisher's Cataloging-in-Publication Data
Geil, Rita.
   Laughing it off : the low-calorie poem diet / Rita Geil. -Flemington, NJ :
   Walnut Pond Press, 2001.

   p. cm.
   ISBN 0-9710953-0-2
   1. Reducing diets-Humor. 2. Weight loss-humor. 3. Humorous poetry.
   I. Title

| PN1083.D54 | 2001 | 2001-091134 |
| G45 2001 | 811.6-dc21 | CIP |

05 04 03 02 01 • 5 4 3 2 1
Illustrations by Athena Thomas • www.athenart.com
Logo design by Paul Stuke Graphics • stuke1943@aol.com

Printed in Singapore

This book is dedicated to
Judy Hoffman

caretaker of the light
from shooting stars

Special Thanks to

Inspirations Hannelore Hahn and the Int'l Women's Writing Guild
Mentors D.H. Melhem, Pat Carr, Myra Shapiro, Susan Tiberghien
Touchstones Ruth Marie Gibbons, IHM, and Ruth Anne Murrray, IHM
Pillars Jill Cunningham, Paul and Bonnie Geil, Matthew Knox, Judy Onystok
Shipmates Gaylen Berse, Diane Fresco, David Frost, Victoria More, Ratna Salana
Wordplayers Kitt Alexander, Marsha L. Browne, Sarah Hile, Jean Zipser
Angels Patti Blair and Annie Shaver-Crandell
Benefactors Lakshmi and Dr. Frederick Lenz
Stewards Kyril and Josephine Dambuleff
and
Friends at the Tuscany Bistro

Contents

* * *

Laughing It Off
The Low-Calorie Poem Diet

Instructions

No special food to try,
or new machines to buy,

    if you have
    some extra weight to rid.

Just read a verse a day,
and laugh the pounds away!

    Well, at least
    you'll feel as if you did!

Liquid Diet Lament

Monday = None Day...
I'll have plain iced tea.

Tuesday = Blues Day...
Veggie broth for me.

Wednesday = Friends Day...
Diet sodas stack.

Thursday = Worst Day...
Pass the coffee, black.

Friday = Sigh Day...
Splurge on Perrier.

Saturday = Flatter Day...
Grapefruit juice okay.

Sunday = Done Day!
(Did I float away?)

New Diet, Day One

This morning
I may look dejected, because
I have suffered a bit of a shock.

Somehow
I have eaten up all today's food,
but it's only eleven o'clock!

Sour Puss

I always thought sour cream looked gross.
               (Its name is also nasty.)

Who would have guessed a thing like that
               would turn out to be tasty?

What irony! When I was thin,
               I wouldn't even try it.

Now that I've grown to love it,
               it's forbidden on my diet!

Going Bananas

Food for Thought

When it comes to romance I take the cake
so the minute I saw him my knees turned to jelly
but I buttered him up
till he was nuts about me
and he said I was the spice of his life
so we were having a peach of a time
until one night he was in a jam
and he told me to get some bread out of his wallet
and sandwiched in between his credit cards
was a cheesecake photo
of another tomato
who thought *she* was his sugar
and that put me in a pickle
so at first I floundered
but then I really stewed
because the apple of my eye
turned out to be a rotten egg
who was full of baloney
and we got into a rhubarb
but he was just a cream puff
and he waffled
when I told him he couldn't cut the mustard
so then I gave him the raspberry and I just walked out
cool as a cucumber

Mary, Mary

Mary, Mary, culinary,
how does your body grow?

> *A bit too muchly, I'm afraid,*
> *with inches all in a row.*

Imagine being flowers!

Then passers-by will say,
not, "Here comes that big lady..."

but

"Here comes that big bouquet!"

One-Foot Exercise

This little piggy did step aerobics.

This little piggy did none.

This little piggy found a workout guru.

This little piggy stayed home
and exercised to videos.

(Which little piggy, do you suppose,
could not fit in new, smaller clothes?)

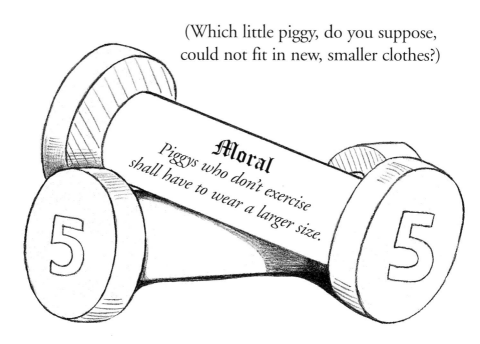

Moral
Piggys who don't exercise
shall have to wear a larger size.

Higher Math

Algebra, and calculus, and trigonometry...
    I avoided them in school, for
    what were they to me?

Now I'm into dieting and, much to my surprise,
    I'm a math whiz just to figure
    how to shrink my size.

Counting calories and fat percentages, to start.
    Then I have to calculate how
    hard to pound my heart.

Working like me with these algorithms, you'll agree:
    Dieting should qualify us
    for a math degree!

Prosecuting Mother Goose

Bo Peep is "little"...

> ...so's Miss Muffet,
> and Jack Horner, too...

> ...plus Polly Flinders,
> Jumping Joan and Jack Jelf,
> and Boy Blue...

> ...and Jenny Wren,
> and Nancy Etticoat...

> (to name a few)

Since I'm *not* little,
I protest Ms. Goose's point of view.

If we took Mother G. to court,
the lawsuit would be sweet:

> Her nursery rhymes discriminate
> in favor of petite!

Ode to a
Reluctant Vegetarian

Little Miss Muffet
decided to tough it
and eat only curds made of soybean.

But along came a spider,
who sat down beside her,
and **WHAP!**

          he was two grams of protein.

Chance Meeting

A fat chance and a thin chance
went out gambling one fine day.

I didn't mean to eavesdrop
but I overheard them say,

"Hey! Hangin' out together
might be problematical,
because between the two of us,
we have no chance at all!"

The Big Fight: Tail o' the Tape
for Bindy

The Gingham Dog and the Calico Cat
got themselves in a famous spat.

I think the Plate (who reported the fight)
didn't quite get all the details right,
omitting the cause of the furious stew,
in short, the *real* reason for the hullabaloo...

(that left the air littered for an hour or so
with bits of gingham and calico...)

> I have it on the very best authority that
> the dog told the cat
> she was getting *too fat.*

Letters to Miss Piggy

Dear Miss Piggy,

Write me back!
I'm a loyal fan.
(You're the best celebrity!)
Help me understand...

I hear that "big is beautiful"
and you sure proved it's true.

How come it doesn't work for me
the way it works for you!

My dear Miss Piggy,

Write again!
I need help from you.
(You're my favorite movie star!)
Tell me what to do...

I long to have your energy,
your style, your enterprise,
your money, fame, and love life.

Well... so far,
I've got your thighs.

Semester Break

No more homework.
  No more books.

No more cafeteria cooks!

40-30-30

I really got excited when
I heard about "the Zone."
It seems to be a way of eating
I can make my own.

At figuring these ratios,
I think I'm doing great!

Wait!

If it's perfect,
how come
there's so little on my plate?

Out to Lunch

Please don't invite me out to eat.
I'm busy losing weight.

It takes all my attention and
I have to concentrate.

I can't afford distractions while
I'm focusing on thin.

Just think of me as *out to lunch*
until lunch is back in!

13 Days of Christmas

On the twelfth day of Christmas
my gourmet gave to me:

twelve donuts dunking,
      eleven pies hot piping,
ten loaves a'browning,
      nine ladles dripping,
eight meats a'mincing,
      seven stews a'simmering,
six geese a'basting,
      five onion rings...
four grilling birds, three French wines,
two turtle soups...
      and a partridge in a pear sauce!

(On the thirteenth day of Christmas
my best friend gave to me:
a diet system gift certificate.)

In the Spirit

I've got the Christmas spirit now!
I know I do, because
I bought a new red velvet dress
and look like Santa Claus.

Christmas Present

Christmas has come over you!
The look becomes you so.

You fairly wear the ancient joy.
I wonder if you know...

You have become a gift yourself,
and all you need's a bow.

19

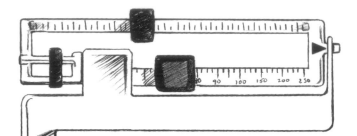

Medical Miracle

I think they should revise that chart
that matches weight and height.

When I locate my "inches tall,"
it says my "pounds" aren't right.

If they *reversed* the columns, though,
at least I could report:

My problem isn't extra weight...
instead, I'm extra short!

Much Too Much

The moment that I hear about
a "guaranteed" new diet,
I feel compelled to rush right out
and buy the stuff to try it.

> The diet doesn't last long, though,
> for pretty soon I've read
> that if I keep on doing it,
> I'll probably drop dead.

It has *too much* preservative
(which pickles up your brains)
or *too much* something else
(a brilliant scientist explains).

> It's much *too much* expensive,
> or it's cheap but *much too* slow,
> or you're drinking *too much* water
> and you always have to go.

There's *too much* controversy and
I'm in a quandary.
The only thing I know for sure is,
there's *too much* of me!

Countdown

Dieting was such a chore...

> I had to be inventive.
> I lost the first ten pounds for Bob,
> but then I lost incentive
> when I lost Bob!
> So much for him.
> I lost the next ten pounds for Jim.

Dieting was such a bore...

> I thought that Chuck would love me more
> if I weighed less.
> (Eight pounds, I guess.)
> Six pounds for Mike,
> and five for Lee.
> Matthew was good for barely three.

Dieting I did abhor...

> I couldn't do it any more,
> not even one for Juan.

Then I caught on...

> ...and lost the rest for me!

Shelf Life

A magazine I read today
described the scientific way
that food is processed anymore,
so bugs won't eat it in the store.

    It mentioned many famous foods,
    reviewing chemicals they use
    to make food last upon the shelf.

So, then I thought about myself...
and why some food that's passed my lips
has ended up right on my hips
and seems determined to remain.

    Now, finally, I can explain
    why weight stays on, once it appears...

    'cause Twinkies last for twenty years!

Economy Class

I'm traveling by airplane and
they're bringing me a meal.
It's brown stuff labeled "gravy,"
on brown stuff labeled "veal."

I'll scarf up every single scrap,
but guilty I won't feel.
I *never* count the calories
when dinner isn't real.

Jiggly Jog

I won't be witnessed jogging down the beach.
    That goal, it's true,
      while it's in view, is still beyond my reach.

I won't be caught in any spandex top!
    The way it shakes,
      the scene it makes is not my photo op.

Until I'm fit, don't bother watching me.
    When I'm in view,
      I'm careful to jog just my memory.

Anniversary

Through all my days of dieting, sweet thing, you've been the cook,

preparing both our meals to help me diet by the book.

Do you recall the marriage vow
we sealed with a kiss?

You swore to stick through thin and thick...

Were you predicting *this*?

Cookbooks

I have a hundred cookbooks, but these days I must resist the urge to be a gourmet. So, I read them with a twist:

I think of them as **screenplays**
with the most delicious plots.

The dialogue is spicy
and the characters are hot!

I love a steamy finish with
the juices running high!

(The trouble with this plot is,
when it thickens...so do I!)

Heaven

Whether or not
I lose a pound
has nothing to do with my grin.

Someday
when I'm an angel
I shall fit on the head of a pin!

Main Squeeze

Can I squeeze into heaven

(though skinny I ain't)

if Oprah Winfrey is my patron saint?

Torture

My notion of hell
(I don't know about you)
is shopping for clothes
with a girlfriend *size 2.*

Phony Baloney

There's been a revolution in the foodstuff marketplace.
Now my refrigerator is a very puzzling place...

Bologna, wrapped in plastic,
looks the way it always looked.

According to the label, though,
it's *turkey*, but it's cooked
some clever way to make me think
it's what it used to be.

Bologna's *really* phony,
now that it's bologna-free!

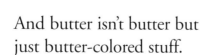

And butter isn't butter but
just butter-colored stuff.

I *can't* believe it's butter...
it's not buttery enough!

The non-fat mayo
makes me think of paste.

I use a dab
to glue together celery
with fabricated crab.

My omelettes are eggless...
my bacon bits are bean.

"New" ice cream is more plastic
than the spoons at Dairy Queen.

The situation's hard to take!

Cheez!
What a lousy deal,
when half the food I eat is fake...
with calories for real!

Broad-Way

I've just seen a marvelous musical, where
I laughed and applauded a lot.

It featured a Rubenesque heroine, which
is why I admired the plot.

The actress wore size 22 at the start...
size 9 when the last curtain fell.

By warbling and whistling her way through the show,
she changed to a true *femme fatale*!

Each song that she sang made her more and more svelte,
from overture right through encore.

Imagine how easy my diet would be,
if only it had a good score!

Check

I see my income tax
and my tax sees me.

Both of us are bigger
than we ought to be.

Futures

I have the *yen* to make the *change*.
I'm *franc* about my weight.

I have the *cents* to diet at
a realistic *rate*.

I've taken very thorough *stock*
to set *marks* I can reach.

This *takeover* has *dividends*
that *yield* upon the beach!

I'm *banking* on my *profile*.
My *interest* abounds.

(But why have I converted all my *assets* into *pounds*?)

Thinking Thin

"Think thin," they say...

They don't say *how* to
practice this fine art,
especially in markets,
loading up my shopping cart
with boxes labeled NEW LARGE SIZE.

I can't "think thin" with ease,
when HEFTY makes my trash bags,
and the GIANT packs my peas!

A Word from Our Sponsor

I had no problems dieting today...

...that is, until
I turned the television on...

> My head began to fill
> with thoughts of pies from Mrs. Smith
> and cakes from Sara Lee
> and fluffy rolls with cinnamon
> and glaze from Pillsbury
> and tacos fresh from Taco Bell,
> Doritos by the score,
> and pizza hot from Pizza Hut
> and hamburgers galore
> from Wendy's and McDonald's, and
> the BK's crispy fries.
> When Baskin Robbins came on screen
> I covered up my eyes!

I know the advertisers pay
for shows I like to see...

but *how* can I lose weight, with those
commercials on TV?

In the Fast Lane

My friend next door lost fifteen pounds,
in just two weeks or so.

Gosh! I lost only five all month,
and still have ten to go!

She told me she's been on a fast...
I guess I'm on a slow.

General Remarks

I fight the Battle of the Bulge:
      One day I starve...
      the next, indulge.

This war is bound to last, I see,
as long as *I'm* my enemy,
      because my pattern of attack
      is three pounds off...
      and two pounds back!

Miss-ing American Pie

And they were singin'...

Bye, bye, any slices of pie.

Drove my Chevy to McDonald's
but the fat was too high.

Them good ol' gals
was drinkin' Slim Fast and rye,
singin' *This'll be the day that I diet...
this'll be the day that I diet...*

The 51st State

If *slender* is a state of mind,
   it's something they should prove.

      (Or tell me where the darn state is,
      so I can promptly move!)

"Daisy, Daisy"

Chris-tie Brink-ley,
give me your diet, do.
I'm half cra-zy
trying to look like you.

I long for your stylish marriage.
I imitate your carriage.

I do look sweet,
though I fill the seat
of a bicycle built for two!

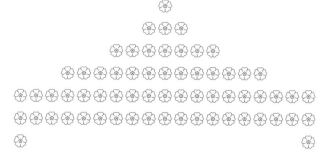

Ample Example

The men in India, they say,
prefer an ample wife.

Why can't I be a sacred cow
and munch my way through life?

Class Reunion

Star light, star bright...

first star I see tonight...

I wish I may...

I wish I might...

lose twenty pounds by tomorrow night...

Chocolate

Friends have been giving me novels to read
when I'm tempted to nibble on treats.
Books will distract me from snacking, they say,
and will save me from savoring sweets.

What is the overall impact on me
that a story can possibly make?
Nobody's written a best seller yet
to compare with a best chocolate cake!

Visualization

At a workshop in visualizing,
I'm picturing myself thin...

How thin...

...as thin as a pretzel...

Oh, no!
Now I'm hungry again!

New Age Jack Sprat

Jack Sprat, who ate no fat,
had a wife who ate no lean.
And so, between the two of them...

      ...they wrote a book,
      and formed a corporation.

      Then they built *Sprat's Flats*,
      where you exercise,
      and they trim your wallet
      while you're trimming your thighs.

      Next they bottled *Jack's Juice*,
      which is just tap water
      that they flavor and sell
      for a dollar and a quarter.

      Now they're touring talk shows
      with *Jumping Jack* machines,
      to help you fit
      in *Le Jacques* designer jeans.

Jack's hair got thin,
from keeping up the pace,
and his wife got
lots of thin lines in her face...

      but what the heck...
      their futures are quite fat!

Science Fiction Illustrated

I'm fond of sci-fi features
and I've seen more than a few.

It's fun to rate strange creatures
by how weird they are to view.

More alien than any
sci-fi creatures I have seen...

...are those bikini models
in that sports fan magazine!

Camping

I can't really claim I go camping.
I don't like to walk very far.
My dream place to spend my vacation
is *not* where the wild things are!

I don't like to get up too early,
be bitten by things in my socks,
or brunch on some tough old beef jerky
with biscuits resembling the rocks.

But though I can't claim I've been camping,
I still feel as if I just went.
Today I tried on a plain brown dress
and thought it would make a good tent.

Lost and Found

My waistline shows I'm losing pounds.
I wonder where they go...

How can those pounds just disappear?
They go *somewhere*, I know.

Suppose lost pounds just float around...
invisible...but there...

What if they wait till someone's still,
then drop down from the air?

The woman next to me at work
is losing steadily.

If I don't keep on moving fast,
her pounds might plop on me!

53

In the Shadow
of Robert Louis Stevenson

I have a friendly shadow who
goes all around with me,
and what can be the use of her
is plain for me to see:

> She shows me
> I can change my shape
> and shift to thin from stout.

> > I'll be a shadow of myself,
> > no shadow of a doubt!

Nutrition Test

When asked to name
the main food groups,
I hopefully assert:

an appetizer,
soup,
a salad,
entrée,
and dessert!

(Whatever groups they use are fine,
so long as they include the wine.)

Fait Accompli

The devil's disguised as a *sous* chef,
a *merveilleux, fantastique* cook
who uses French menus to tempt me.

I'm hell-bound the moment I look!

There's always a sauce made with fine wine,
or caviar, vodka, and brie.
A French sauce just can't be resisted!

My fate is a fat *accompli*!

Rainbow Sherbet

Rainbow Sherbet!
Watercolors in the ice cream shoppe...
        orange and grape and apricot,
        lime and lemon drop.

Renoir would faint
if he beheld pistachio, or peach.

        Picasso would be passionate
        to paint with pumpkin,
        each bright splash of flavor!

How Monet of me to savor
peppermint and wild cherry, mandarin and boysenberry.

        I'm Degas,
        swirling toffee just like sepia in my dish.

I'm quite Gauguin with melon ice...
        Toulouse-Lautrec, with licorice.

Like a painter
I have canvassed ice cream parlors, north and south.

        My palette is that of an *artiste*...
        It just happens to be in my mouth!

Mirror, Mirror

there are days
    I feel so thin
    I fear the wind will take me

then

    walking past a looking glass
    I marvel at my size

      I wear a thin disguise

Dialogue

Perhaps I have a fat soul...

I'll ask,
and hear the answer:

Oh, soul...
are you a fat soul?

No, dear.
I am a dancer.

Unseasoned Haiku

1

Old friends at dinner,
intimate conversation.
Such good nourishment.

2

A taste for beauty,
a hunger for adventure.
A large appetite.

3

Meal like a painting:
color, texture, form, and line.
Master chef at work.

4

Fourteen diet books,
ten years and twenty diets.
Time to lighten up!

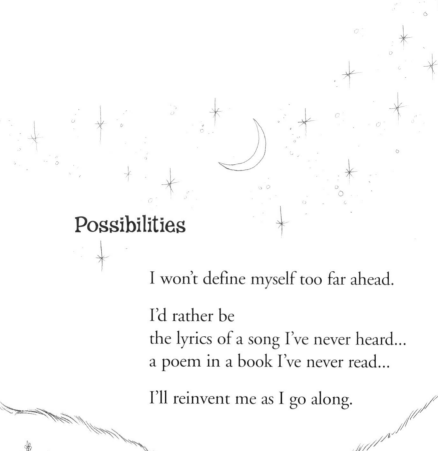

Possibilities

I won't define myself too far ahead.

I'd rather be
the lyrics of a song I've never heard...
a poem in a book I've never read...

I'll reinvent me as I go along.

Alternatives

Couch Potato

One, two...
                    (Nothing to do)
Three, four...
                    (Eat some more)
Five, six...
                    (Watching flicks)
Seven, eight...
                    (Pick up weight)
Nine, ten...
                    (Diet again)

Hot Potato

One, two...
          (Lifestyle review)

Three, four...
              (Exercise more)

Five, six...
              (Pilates kicks)

Seven, eight...
              (Posture straight)

9 / 10
          (My size again!)

Overview

I'm...
> over thirty,
> overweight,
> overanxious, too.

> My bank account is overdrawn.
> My raise is overdue.

I overstate the case because
I'm overwhelmed today.

> But overall,
> I'm overjoyed,
> for change is underway!

The New Me

Grand Opening Universe!

Don't miss this big event!
Stars will make their appearance, directly above the main tent!

Offer good today only!
See the banner of life unfurled!

Free admission!
Free entertainment!

Take a chance!
Win a ride on the world!

Our web site

will be ready for you by June, 2002.

* * *

See you then!

www.laughingitoff.com

How to Keep
Laughing It Off

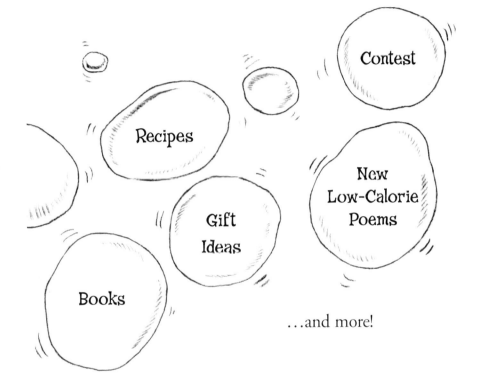

Contest

Recipes

New
Low-Calorie
Poems

Gift
Ideas

Books

…and more!

Visit our web site

www.laughingitoff.com

Walnut Pond Press, 203 Main Street #325, Flemington NJ 08822

RAISE $$$

for your organization with

Laughing It Off

low-calorie events!

Poems • Music • Comedy

Book signings

Book discounts for groups

www.laughingitoff.com